COLIN WHITTOCK

The Perils of Moving House

For Daddy.
Merry xmas
+ I hope you
enjoy this book
↓ you
can
certainly
identify with it!
lots of love
- em ♥

CENTURY
LONDON MELBOURNE AUCKLAND JOHANNESBURG

First published in 1987 by Century Hutchinson Ltd,
Brookmount House, 62–65 Chandos Place, Covent Garden,
London WC2N 4NW

Century Hutchinson Australia Pty Ltd,
PO Box 496, 16–22 Church Street, Hawthorn, Victoria 3122,
Australia

Century Hutchinson New Zealand Ltd,
PO Box 40–086, Glenfield, Auckland 10,
New Zealand

Century Hutchinson South Africa Pty Ltd,
PO Box 337, Bergvlei, 2012 South Africa

ISBN 0 7126 1789 2

Filmset by Deltatype,
Ellesmere Port

Printed in Great Britain by R.J. Acford, Chichester

Why Move?

Maybe your present home is too big. . .

*I said, now the children have gone, perhaps
we should buy something a little smaller.*

or too small. . .

We could do with another room.

or the garden is becoming more than you can handle.

A crazy-paved window box would suit me!

**It may be better circumstances –
promotion, for instance. . .**

But we'd be going up in the world.

Then, of course, it could be awkward neighbours. . .

We're so sorry you're going.

*That sounds like a good programme – shall
we put our TV on?*

and move on.

I've left you enough room to get out this time. . .

Not that it's always malicious. . .

*I said, I thought it was sweet of them to offer
to dedicate their next 4-day reggae party to
our leaving the flat!*

Sometimes it's because you can do no more to your present property. . .

*Planning permission? Did we get **what** planning permission?*

Or the relationship may be breaking up. . .

Hold on a sec – I'll see if I can organize a truce.

And sometimes it's quite out of your control. . .

George, you know you thought you heard banging?

It may be retirement to a different area. . .

*Don't do it mate – can't move in the summer
and a bloody ghost-town in winter!*

Or it may simply be cheaper in the long run!

Selling

**Nowadays some people try to sell
without any help by placing an ad in the
local paper. . .**

*Just another Estate Agent offering to sell it
for us!*

– but it can lead to difficulties when buying your next property.

*Pity you can't use our 'Sell-and-Buy'
package. . .*

Most, however, still use that special breed – the Estate Agent. . .

Mummy and Daddy, this is Michael. He's an Estate Agent – but he's not really like that!

I've just read the agent's details of our house – do you really think we ought to go?

and patiently excuses. . .

It's bad at the moment – we're coming out of the winter wind-down into the summer slump.

the slowness of your sale.

*Somebody somewhere is searching
desperately for a property just like yours. . .*

Then, of course, the children have to be told. . .

*But I **love** my tiny bedroom!*

which can be upsetting. . .

*Teddy **doesn't want** to move!*

embarrassing. . .

*Nobody **leaves** the Black Hand Gang!*

and devastating.

Doris Mainwaring can still come and visit us.

However, they usually accept the situation once they've got it out of their systems.

But I've lived here all my life. . .

Enter the househunters, who come in many forms: – the downright nosey. . .

*We're **not** selling the contents!*

the aspiring. . .

Thanks for showing us round – we really hope we can afford something like this one day.

the muddy. . .

Well, there's nowhere for the dog for a start!

the first-time buyer. . .

How much did you pay when you were our age?

the gushers. . .

Absolutely sooper, the decorations are perfect, we could put our furniture straight in, so near to the schools and shops, what a pretty bathroom, marvellous, what a wonderful kitchen, far more than we dared hope for, you would be prepared to leave the curtains and carpets, so much better than anything else we've seen. . .

Oh, how quaint – it's like that little kitchen we had in our first house!

the expert. . .

Did you know you had Anobium punctatum?*

*woodworm

the casual passers-by. . .

C'mon luv – it's stopped raining.

the unusual. . .

the gullible . . .

*He said he couldn't sell the house to just anybody –
but he really likes us . . .*

Try to look beyond the awful colours and hideous furnishings.

Eventually an offer is made. . .

*Oh yes, **lots** of people are **very** interested!*

– and it's often the people who appear least interested who bid.

Well, we've got to live somewhere. . .

**Of course, this usually triggers a
last-minute rush. . .**

Pity. . .we'd have paid the full amount.

Buying

So, it is time to buy. . .

*Good grief! Either we're grossly underpriced
or these are all grossly overpriced!*

It's quite common nowadays to sell before you begin to look for a new house. . .

We'll never find anything – there's nothing, there's absolutely nothing worth moving to!

Some want smaller properties. . .

But where will the grandchildren sleep?

You must look for faults. . .

I spotted the damp patch because we're hiding the same problem.

and form your own opinions about room sizes.

It's very cosy in the winter!

Always check for local amenities. . .

Where's the nearest pub?

and be prepared for other people's foibles.

. . . and we'll be leaving Arthur's built-in stuffed-bird collection.

The real skill is in looking beyond other people's ideas on furnishing. . .

We've always found this a nice room.

*Fifteen hundred quid, I was quoted, but I put
it in for £750.*

and decorations.

This wallpaper cost 40 quid a roll.

Don't be pushed into a decision.

We're open to offers!. . .

Think about important matters like security. . .

'Ere, who's nicked our burglar alarm?

and remember that long frontages or side fences with tree screens which can look gorgeous in summer. . .

It's all ours. . .

need maintaining. . .

You ought to be ashamed – your fence is an eyesore!

'The autumn leaves. . .'

You should also check running costs. . .

Allowed two dustbins? We won't be able to afford to throw anything away.

– including everything. . .

*His central heating bills were more than our
present mortgage!*

But eventually you will find your dreamhouse, which usually comes in one of two forms – 'with potential'. . .

Of course, it needs a little attention.

or expensive. . .

You'll be clear by the time you're 75.

It's useful to obtain a surveyor's report. . .

. . . otherwise it's fine!

But the most expertise is shown in their terms of engagement, which mean they can't be blamed for anything they miss!

So it's time to raise the finance.

*How far beyond our means are you prepared
to let us go?*

Some prefer to go to their bank. . .

Well, you own everything else I have.

Others look to their insurance broker for better long-term returns.

A pension mortgage is best, but we'd have to give up a few little luxuries like eating and drinking. . .

By this time you'll have contacted your solicitor. . .

*You know, of course, about the new by-pass,
the pig-farm and the mining subsidence?*

who is meant to search and warn.

There's a covenant on the property preventing you from converting it either into a pub or a brothel. . .

They negotiate dates and clear up any hiccups

It seems all right for the 10th, but some idiot 8 links down the chain is threatening to pull out. . .

*All part of the service. Only too pleased to
help. Now, it was a bridging loan of £45,000
for two days at. . .*

Sometimes solicitors are blamed for slowing down the transaction. . .

Yes, I have your papers in front of me at the moment.

But at least you can sleep at night knowing you are legally bound.

Don't worry, dear, I'm sure we'll manage somehow!

A word on Scotland, which is different. . .

Sealed bids are submitted against a guide figure. . .

Do you think we ought to add another couple of thousand?

**and the accepted bid is agreed absolute
– thus preventing gazumping.**

*Congratulations – it's yours now, whether ye
want it or no!*

**The Scottish system is said to be better –
especially by surveyors. . .**

*Aye, ah ken ye've had 7 surveys tae date,
MacStraiton, and no bought a hoose!*

And then, of course, there are the yuppies. . .

The yuppie's skill is in spotting a run-down area which is ready for upgrading. . .

It's simply perfect – the houses are crumbling, I was mugged twice and accosted 6 times.

They then try to buy cheaply. . .

*Leave this to me. How much are you asking
for this run-down old shack?*

– which doesn't always work as folk become more aware. . .

Offers over £150,000!

But when they move in they 'improve' the property and the area.

They try to blend with existing neighbours. . .

From the front it looks like a bookshop, but inside you'll find the finest Patagonian cuisine around!

and property values begin to soar.

*So far, its value would buy us a mansion in
Worcestershire, a pied-à-terre in town and,
by next Tuesday, a villa in Marbella.*

**And when the area has become
gentrified they move to the country. . .**

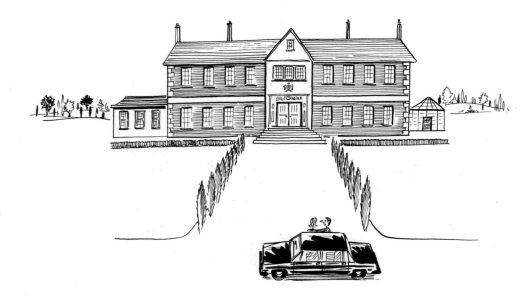

*We can have it for the same price as our
3-bedroomed town house in Mayfair.*

get bored. . .

*We'll have to go back – you're beginning to
sound like Walter Gabriel.*

and then hope they'll be able to raise enough to return to London to find another run-down area where they can . . . buy . . . cheaply . . . and . . .

The Move

Can we throw away the pram?

Everybody agrees one of the bonuses of house moving is the chance of a good clear-out. . .

You're not really taking 5 years' worth of Dandy and Beano with you?

Services have to be disconnected. . .

Shall I read the meter now or after you've made me a cup of tea?

and re-connected.

*At least you're a shareholder in a company
that gets paid for doing nothing...*

The removal men are generally cheerful British workmen with great skill. . .

Leave everything to us, mate.

You carry on – don't worry about my back, I'll be all right.

Got a grand piano out of a loft once.

although some householders don't help as much as others.

Right! You can start where you like. . .

They have an incredible ability to lift. . .

Hang on! I'm still sorting stuff out!

I think I liked it better upstairs in our bedroom.

– sometimes.

On the plus-side, we'll be able to get your dining table in through it!

You pray that all dates and appointments will be kept. . .

(sometimes the old tenant can be pedantic. . .)

No, no, let's do it properly – I'll take my keys to my solicitor, who will hand them to your solicitor, who will hand them to you.

and you hope that they've left their house in as clean and tidy a condition as you have left yours. . .

*Have they left **what** light bulbs in **what** light sockets?*

A little petulance can creep in. . .

So much for your 'I'll soon sort out those removal men'!

and the unthinking remark can hurt. . .

What time will dinner be ready?

I thought a nice casserole might be welcome.

Of course, you pray your new neighbours will be as nice as the last. . .

I was hoping to borrow a better lawnmower than that.

and begin to get to know them as soon as possible.

*They're **all** yours?*

Some are a bit too talkative. . .

Is that you, Tom – did I tell you about the trouble I had with my car?

And it isn't always wise to reveal your occupation. . .

I understand your husband is a plumber?

But you soon get to know them and work at getting on.

I think I have something that belongs to you!

Pets also have to adapt and establish their new territory. . .

They said we shouldn't let him out for a few weeks.

and some prefer their old patch. . .

Your dog's found his way back again.

And then it takes a while for the post to settle down.

Twelve for them and one bill for us!

But the kids soon appreciate their new home.

You said my bigger bedroom would mean I could have my friends in. . .

Other temptations may intrude. . .

Sod it! Let's move to a flat and buy one of these.

But it's all worth it in the end – until the next time. . .

In 6 years 11 months 3 weeks and 6 days we'll be off again!